THE OFFICIAL WORKBOOK
MINECRAFT
GRADE 1

Written by Russell Ginns
Illustrations by Antonio Vecchione

WELCOME TO A LEARNING ADVENTURE!

This workbook lets kids practice essential skills while taking a journey through the world of Minecraft. Learn skip counting while building a house and vowel blends while crafting tools! There are dozens of activities filled with reading, math, and critical-thinking skills, all set among the biomes, mobs, and loot of your child's favorite game.

Special Minecraft Missions at the end of each lesson also send readers on learning challenges inside and outside the book!

Here are some tips to make the most of this workbook:

- Make sure your child has a quiet, comfortable place to work.

- Give your child a variety of pencils, crayons, and any other items they may need to write answers, draw pictures, or set up games.

- Read the directions with your child. There's a lot of information and adventures packed into each chapter! You can help tell the stories and point out the basic tasks that need to be done.

- Spend extra time on any section that your child finds difficult.

- Enjoy the fun Minecraft facts and jokes with your child. This is your chance to learn more about a game that interests them!

Grab a pen or pencil and get ready to have fun as you learn with Minecraft!

TIME TO EXPLORE

You've arrived in the world of Minecraft. Start out by exploring your surroundings.

In this adventure, you will...

Explore the terrain.

Gather wood.

Make a crafting table.

Use wood tools.

Let's get started!

BUILDING WORDS

Explore some of your surroundings in the world.

Draw a line between matching flowers. Then write the word that each pair spells.

PLA   Y   _____

JUN   TER   _____

WA   UN   _____

SK   GLE   _____

S   EAN   _____

OC   INS   _____

MINECRAFT FACT: Forests, plains, oceans, and mountains are some of the most common biomes in Minecraft.

4

Add a pair of double letters to finish each word.

Use these letter pairs:

ss   oo   ee   rr   nn

tr__

ru__ing

pa__ot

gra__

cr__per

wi__er

bamb__

You did it! Place your sticker here.

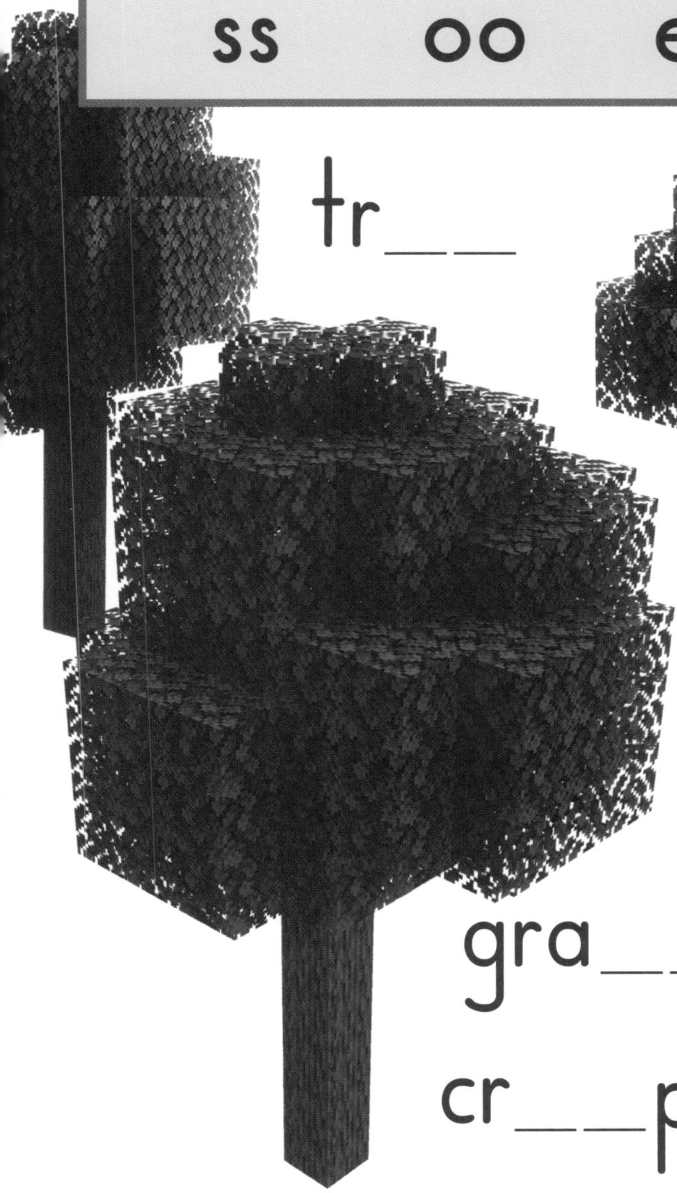

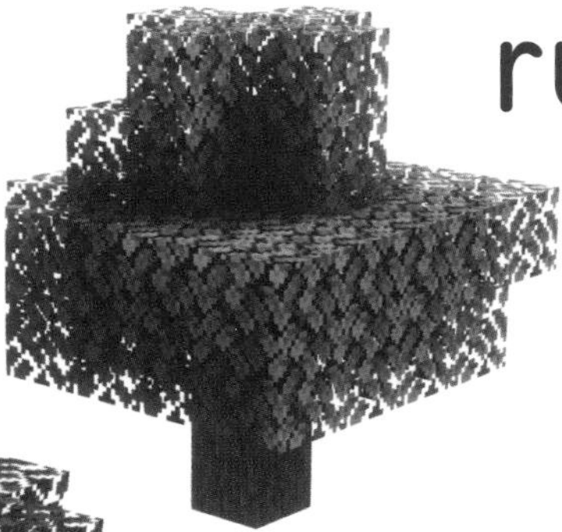

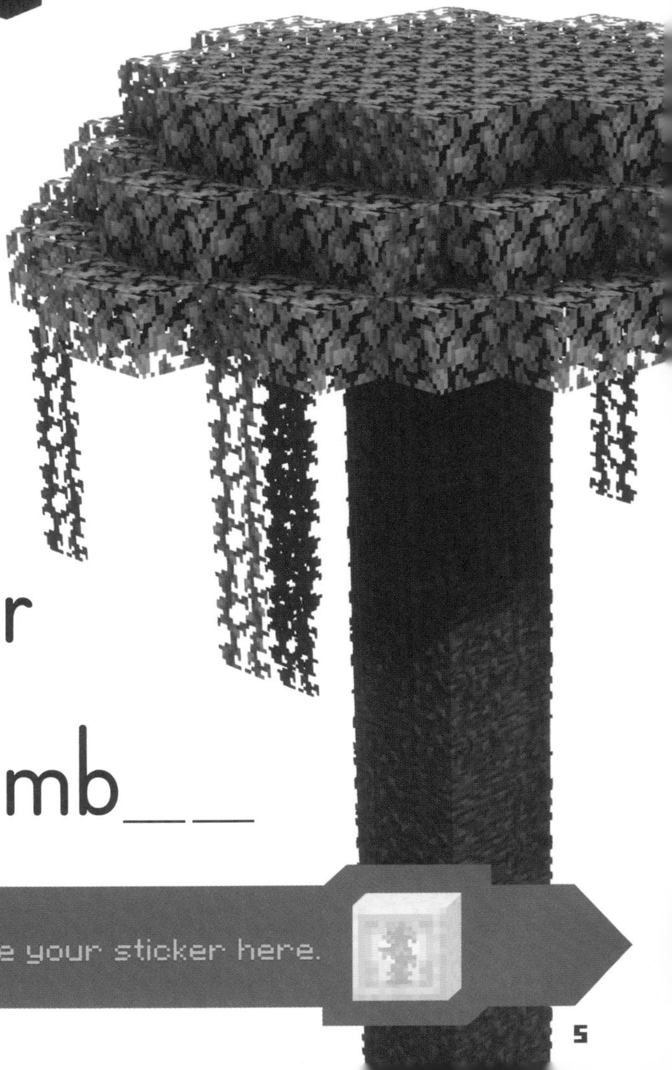

Break trees to gather wood so you can craft them into planks.

Add **st** or **sl** to each set of blocks to make a word.

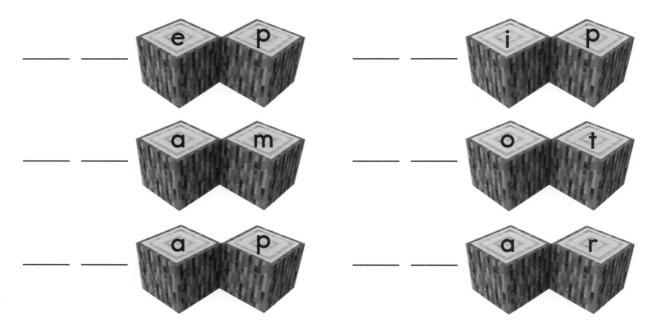

Add **fl** or **fr** to each set of blocks to make a word.

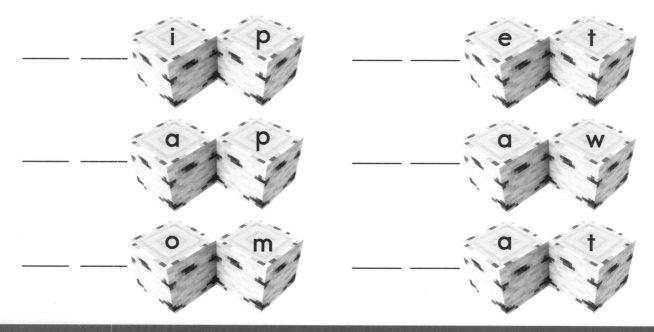

Write the word next to each pair of planks.

 _____

 _____

 _____

 _____

 _____

 _____

 _____

 _____

 _____

 _____

 _____

 _____

It takes wood to make a crafting table. You'll use that to build tools and a lot of other useful things in Minecraft.

Add **est** or **ast** to each plank to make a word.

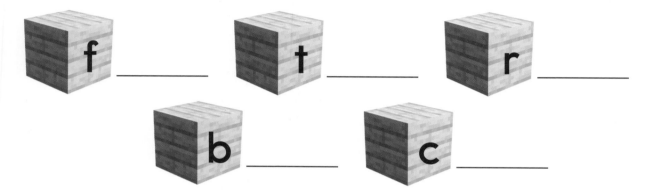

f _____   t _____   r _____

b _____   c _____

Add **ilk** or **elt** to each plank to make a word.

b _____   s _____   f _____

Add **art** or **ark** to each plank to make a word.

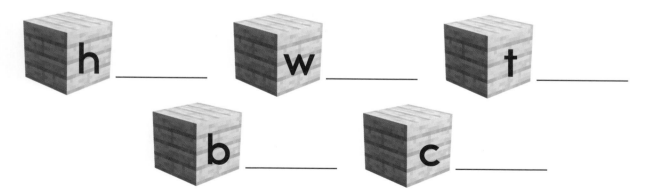

h _____   w _____   t _____

b _____   c _____

MINECRAFT FACT: Wood tools are usually the first type of items you will craft to advance in the world.

Unscramble each group of letters to form a real word, then write it.

V		T
A		R
E		L

➡️ TRAVEL

T		L
A		K

➡️ TALK

		A
		W
L		K

➡️ WALK

S		I
F		I
H		N

➡️ FINISH

Use your wood tools to help you collect different resources.

Use your pickaxe and draw a **circle** (O) around the **stone** (⬛) and **ore** (⬛).

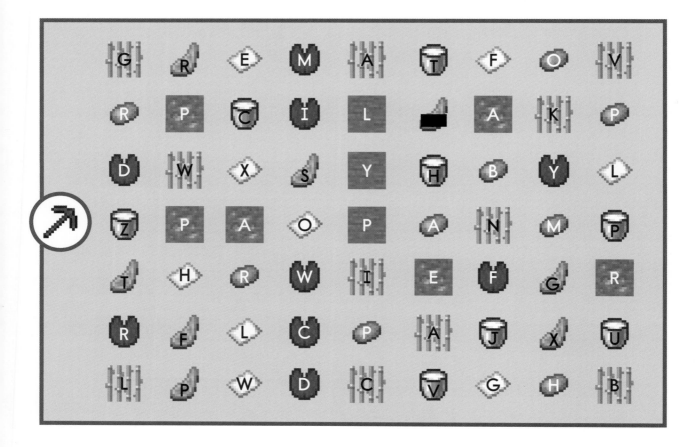

Now write the letters that you circled in the spaces below to form words. (Hint: They are already in the correct order.)

__ __ __ __   __ __ __ __ __

What should you say when you're leaving a nice Minecraft environment?
"Goodbye-omes!"

Use your shovel and draw a **circle** (O) around the **dirt** (▨), **sand** (▨), and **gravel** (▨). Then write the letters that you circled in the spaces below to form words.

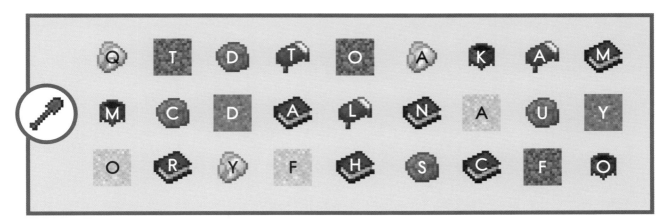

__ __ __ __ __   __ __ __

Use your axe and draw a **circle** (O) around the **wood** (▨ ▨ ▨). Then write the letters that you circled in the spaces below to form words.

__ __ __   __ __ __

MINECRAFT MISSION

Now that you've learned a bit about the world of Minecraft, explore *your* world with a special challenge.

This mission sends you *outside* of this book! Your task is to explore the different regions of your house in search of five items that fit these rules:

- Something that starts with the letters **str**
- Something that ends with the letters **ate**
- Something that contains a pair of double letters
- Something that starts with the letters **br**
- Something that ends with the letters **ilk**

Write the items you find on the lines below, and have an adult check your work. Then find the correct sticker and place it in the lower corner. You've completed your first mission!

_____   _____

_____   _____

_____

MINECRAFT EXPLORE

Great job! You earned a badge! Place your sticker here.

HOME, SWEET HOME

A house will protect you from mobs. You should build one right away!

In this adventure, you will...

Collect tools.

Smelt bricks.

Stack blocks.

Build walls.

Let's get started!

You'll need to collect tools to build your house.

Draw a **square** (□) around every **pickaxe** (⚒).

How many **pickaxes** (⚒) are in your inventory? _____

Now draw a **circle** (○) around every **shovel** (🔨).

How many **shovels** (🔨) are in your inventory? _____

MINECRAFT FACT: A pickaxe is a very important tool in Minecraft.

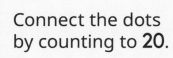

Connect the dots by counting to **20**.

5 6
7 8
4 9
3 10
14
2 15
16
18 17
1 11
20 19 13 12

Count the axes, and write how many are in each group.

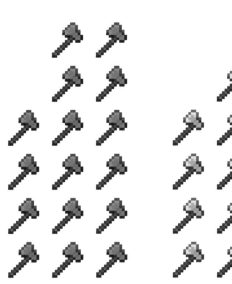

_____   _____   _____   _____

You found lots of clay balls. Use them to make bricks by smelting them in a furnace.

Write what comes before and after each number. The first one has been done for you.

22   23   24

75

31

102

55

68

96

114

62

47

89

119

MINECRAFT FACT: A crafting table can be used to repair damaged items.

16

Craft your bricks into a block of bricks on a crafting table.

Fill in the missing numbers, counting from 1 to 120.

1		3		5	6		8		10
11	12			15		17			20
	22	23			26		28		30
31			34	35		37			40
	42		44		46		48	49	
51	52			55		57		59	
61			64	65		67			70
	72	73			76		78		
81				85	86		88		90
	92	93			96		98		100
101			104	105		107			
	112			115			118		120

You did it! Place your sticker here.

While digging for materials to build your house, you collected stacks of blocks!

Write the number of **hundreds**, **tens**, and **ones** under each set. The first one has been done for you.

189

Hundreds: 1

Tens: 8

Ones: 9

231

Hundreds: _____

Tens: _____

Ones: _____

743

Hundreds: _____

Tens: _____

Ones: _____

MINECRAFT FACT: The Minecraft world contains over 820 different blocks.

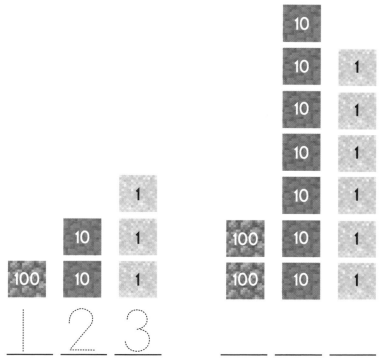

Count the number of blocks in each **hundreds**, **tens**, and **ones** stack. Then write the number below and read the full value aloud. The first one has been done for you.

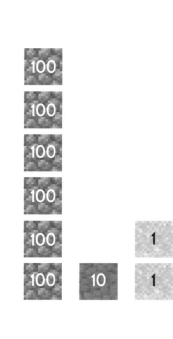

_1_ _2_ _3_   ___ ___ ___   ___ ___ ___

Careful! These blocks are all mixed up. Count them and write the total values below.

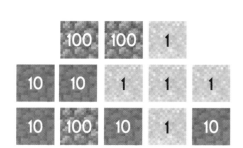

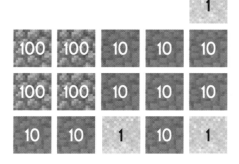

___ ___ ___   ___ ___ ___

You will need brick blocks to build the walls of your house.
Count how many are in your inventory.

Fill in all the missing numbers to skip count by **threes**. The first one has
been done for you.

| 1 | 2 | 3 | 4 | 5 | | 7 | 8 | | 10 | 11 | | 13 | 14 |

| | 26 | 25 | | 23 | 22 | | 20 | 19 | | 17 | 16 |

Now skip count by **fives**.

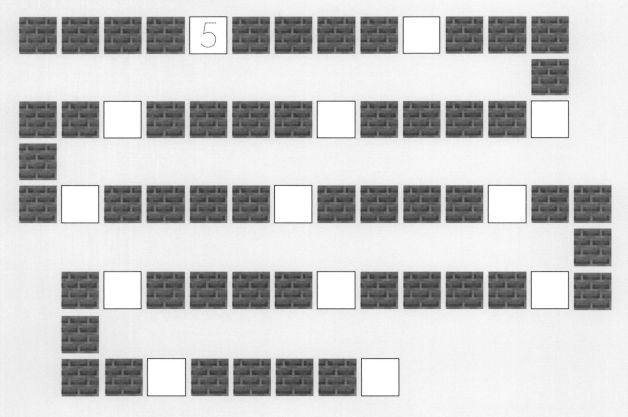

| | | | | 5 | | | | | | | |

Knock, knock. Who's there? *Dan.* Dan who? *Dan-ger! Zombies are coming!*

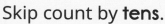

Skip count by **tens**.

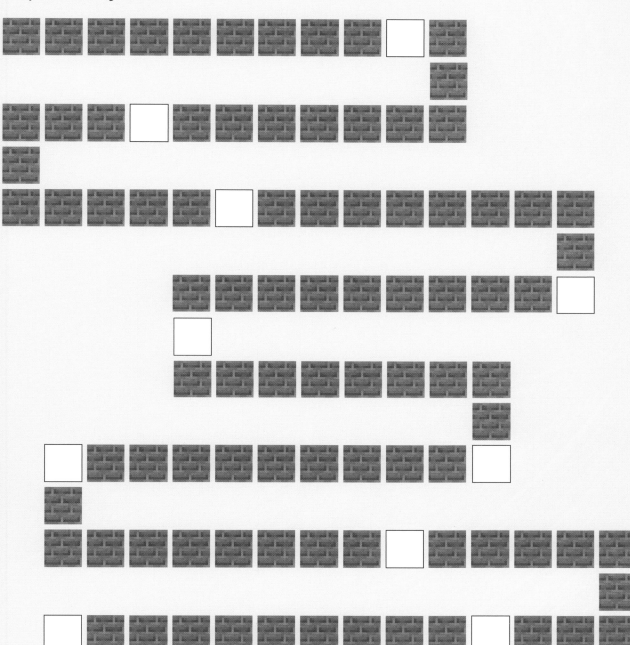

How many total blocks are on these two pages? _____

MINECRAFT MISSION

You've built a house to keep you safe. Now go on a mission to decorate your new place.

This mission sends you on a search *inside* this book. There are items hidden in the top borders of most pages!

Write the page number where you find each one. The first one has been done for you.

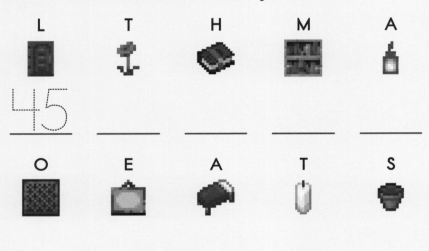

L	T	H	M	A
45	___	___	___	___

O	E	A	T	S
___	___	___	___	___

Write the letter above each item in order of smallest to largest page number.

___ ___ ___

___ ___ ___ ___

MINECRAFT BUILD

Great job! You earned a badge! Place your sticker here.

SURVIVE THE NIGHT

There are mobs everywhere! Avoid them to survive through a whole night.

In this adventure, you will...

Run from zombies.

Patch holes.

Escape from creepers.

Clear away dangers.

Let's get started!

You were out gathering supplies when mobs spotted you. Run away!

Draw a line to connect pairs of words. The second word should be spelled the same as the first word, except with an **e** at the end.

cap	hope
hop	fine
tap	tote
fin	note
pin	tape
not	cape
tot	pine

Now say the words in each pair. Notice how an **e** changes things?

MINECRAFT FACT: Keep energized with food, and you'll be able to outrun most mobs.

Find a path from **START** to **END**. You can only pass through words that end in **e**.

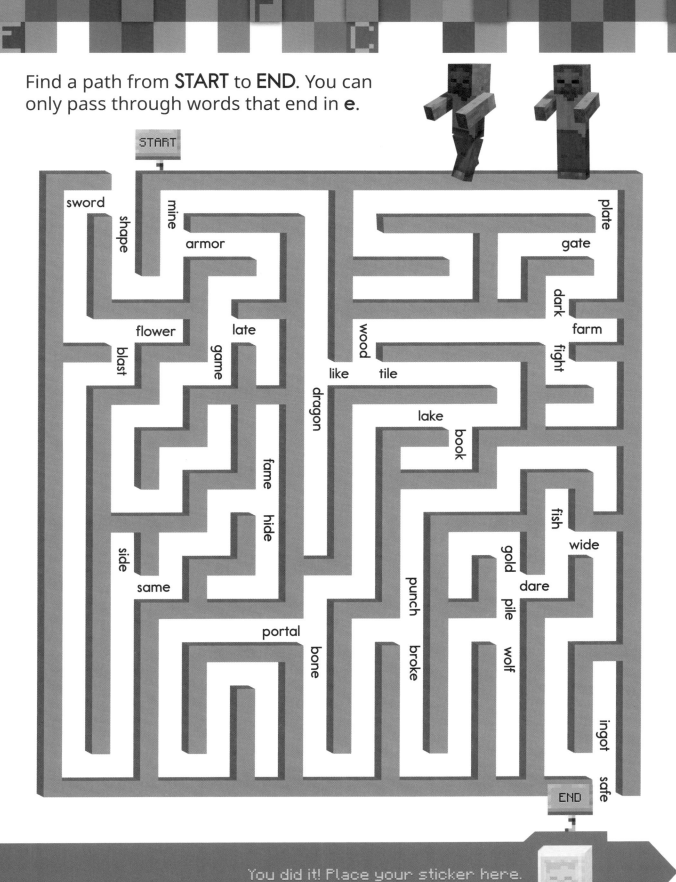

START

sword
shape
mine
armor
plate
gate
dark
farm
fight
flower
late
wood
game
blast
like
tile
dragon
lake
book
fame
hide
fish
wide
side
same
gold
pile
dare
wolf
portal
bone
punch
broke
ingot
safe
END

DOUBLE VOWELS

Creepers are everywhere, and some have exploded! Patch all the holes to make the ground smooth so you can escape.

Patch holes to make a path from **START** to **END**. You can only patch holes that contain words with **double vowels**.

START

feet
speed
dig

steal
ore
food

team

real
keep

wet

off
bread
smelt

eye
meat

MINECRAFT FACT: Jump over holes or patch them! If you fall in one, you might take damage.

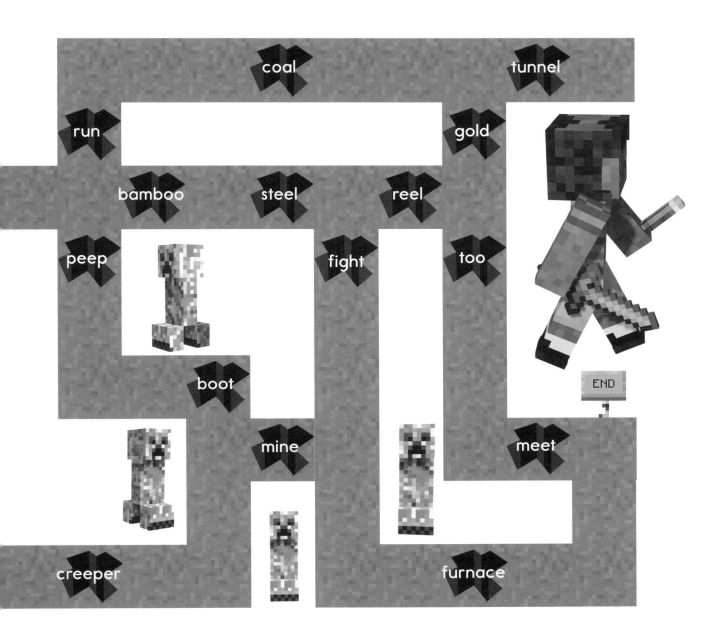

coal

tunnel

run

gold

bamboo

steel

reel

peep

fight

too

END

boot

mine

meet

creeper

furnace

Can you think of two more words with double vowels?

_____   _____

You did it! Place your sticker here.   TNT

27

Stay hidden as you move toward the getaway boats.

Circle all the words that have the letters **ea**.

beach

trees

block

team

chase

steal

water

fight

hide

heat

boat

MINECRAFT FACT: *Creepers that can't see you won't ignite.*

Circle all the boats that only have **oa** words.

goal   road   pond

loaf   toll   goat

soap   coal   boat

moat   coat   moan

gold   cold   oats

How many total
oa words are there on
the boats on this page? _____

Your house is just past these trees. Clear all the nearby zombies so you can get home safe and sound.

Color every letter that does not have a zombie inside it. Read only the colored letters and write them in order in the spaces on page 31.

Then read what you've written to discover a message!

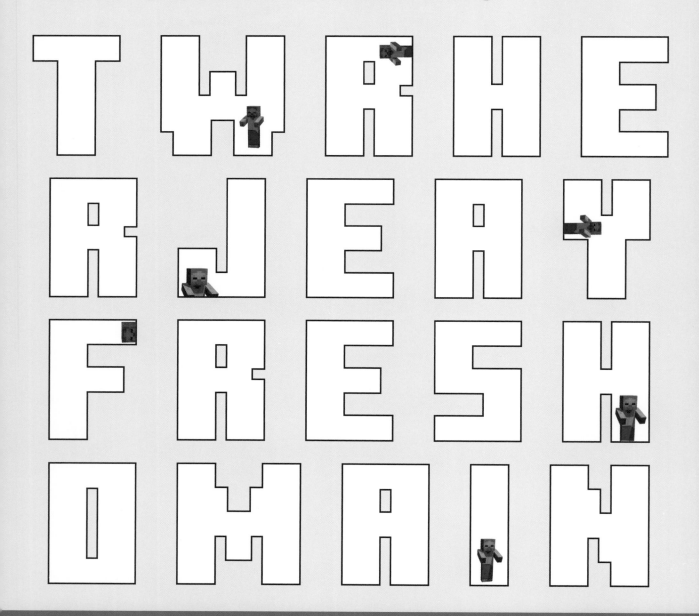

What kind of handbag is full of mobs? A cree-purse!

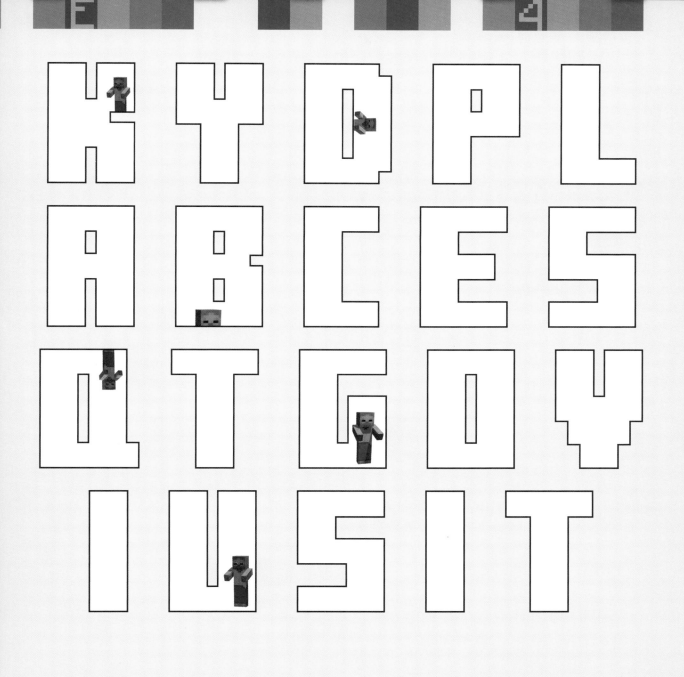

K Y D P L

A B C E S

D T G O V

I U S I T

_ _ _ _ _ _ _ _ _ _ _ _ _ _ _ _ _ _ _

_ _ _ _ _ _ _ _ _ _ _ _

MINECRAFT MISSION

You're back in your snug and cozy home. Make your room in real life a special place to stay.

This mission is a project *outside* of this book! Decorate your room with art that uses some words from this adventure.

You'll need:

- Crayons
- Paper
- Pencils
- Scissors
- Tape

Make a poster, a door hanger, and some labels or signs for your favorite things. Here's the catch: you must use at least two words with **silent e** and two with **double vowels**.

Write the words you used below.

_____   _____

_____   _____

MINECRAFT SURVIVE

Great job! You earned a badge! Place your sticker here.

WELCOME TO THE MOUNTAINS

There are resources in the mountains. Look for canyons, mineshafts, and caves.

In this adventure, you will...

Look for ore.

Descend into a canyon.

Find a mineshaft.

Explore tunnels.

Let's get started!

You've located a canyon. It's a good place to look for veins of ore.

Draw a **circle** (○) around all the ore that has an **addition** (+) symbol.
Draw a **square** (□) around all the ore that has a **subtraction** (-) symbol.

+	&	+	=	-	+	+	+	=	+
+	+	-	+	-	$	=	+	÷	×
-	+	÷	+	+	-	-	+	$	-
+	×	-	&	+	-	+	@	-	+
÷	-	÷	-	-	=	+	+	&	-
+	&	×	+	@	+	-	÷	=	+
+	$	-	+	+	÷	+	-	+	$
+	@	-	-	×	×	&	+	+	-
-	+	@	+	-	+	=	+	×	-

How many **addition** (+) symbols did you find? _____

How many **subtraction** (-) symbols did you find? _____

MINECRAFT FACT: Canyons often open into larger caves filled with resources.

Cross out every block of ore that does NOT have an **addition (+)**, **subtraction (-)**, or **equals (=)** symbol.

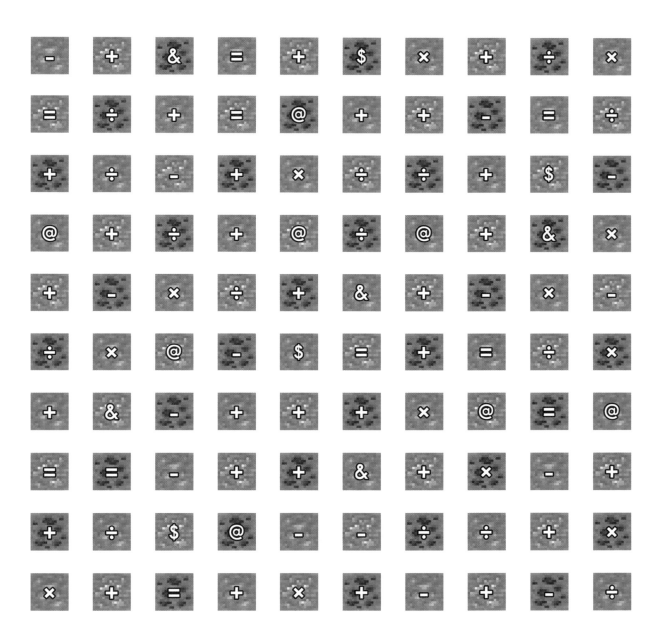

How many **equals (=)** symbols are on this page? _____

Descend into the canyon. Avoid falling into lava on your way down.

Find a safe path through this canyon from **START** to **END**. Solve the lava problems as you go. WARNING: You can only climb over lava problems that add up to a total of **10** or less.

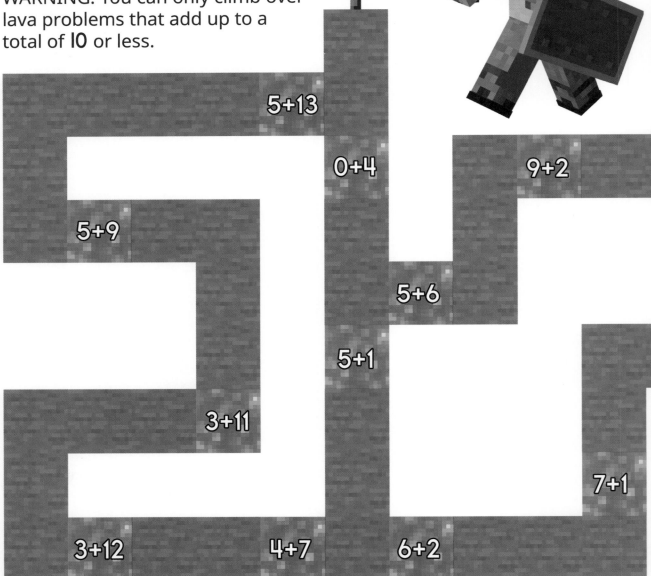

START

5+13

0+4

9+2

5+9

5+6

5+1

3+11

7+1

3+12

4+7

6+2

MINECRAFT FACT: A canyon can be more than 50 blocks deep.

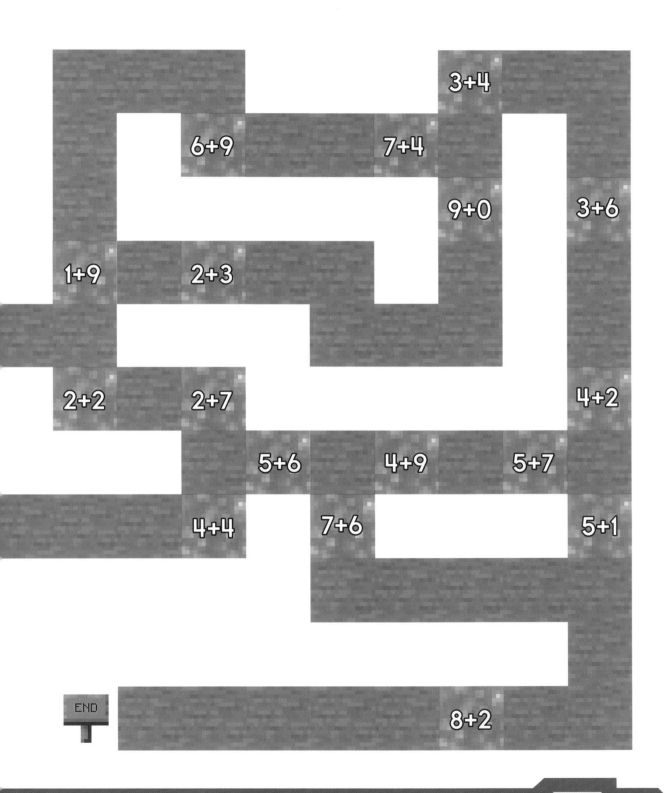

3+4

6+9　　　7+4

9+0　　3+6

1+9　2+3

2+2　2+7

4+2

5+6　4+9　5+7

4+4　7+6

5+1

END

8+2

You did it! Place your sticker here.

You've found mineshafts. Grab a torch and explore.

Each time you pass a cave spider, subtract its value from the number below your torch. Write the final value at the end of each tunnel.

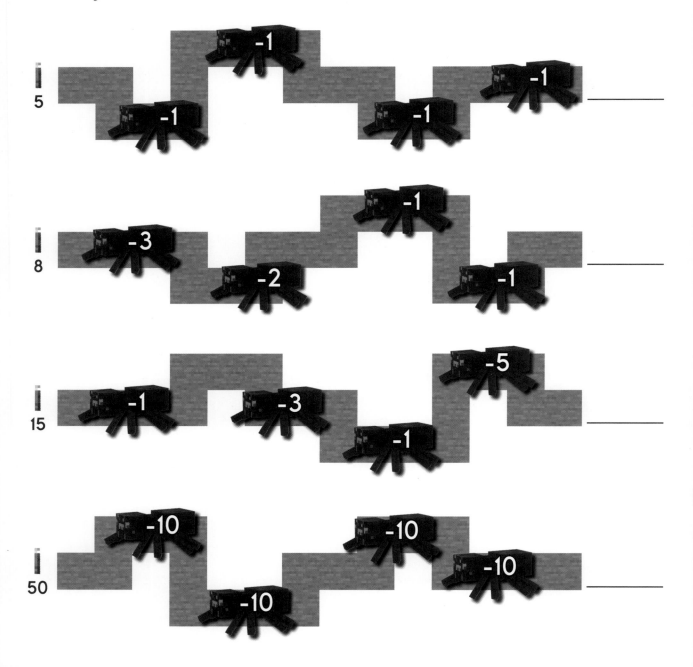

Climb down these mineshafts and subtract as you go. Write the value at the bottom of each one.

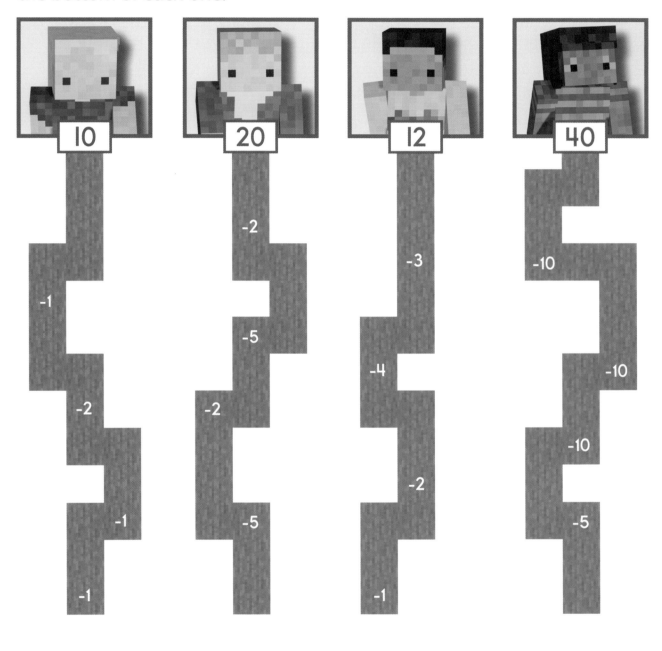

| 10 | 20 | 12 | 40 |

-1   -2   -3   -10

-2   -5   -4   -10

-1   -2   -2   -10

-1   -5   -1   -5

_____ _____ _____ _____

Circle the explorer of the mineshaft with the lowest value.

You did it! Place your sticker here.

You're almost there! Ride a minecart to reach the end of the tunnel.

Here's a super challenge! Start with the number **25**, and draw a path to reach the end of the tunnel. **Add** if you reach a **chest** (🗃). **Subtract** if you reach a **cave spider** (🕷). Try to get all the way from **START** to **END** without reaching **0**.

Keep track of your number as you go. There is space to do so in the box to the right.

If your number reaches 0, start over! Can you make it in less than three tries? (Hint: There is more than one correct path.)

What did Steve say when he discovered a tunnel full of treasure?   *"Mine!"*

40

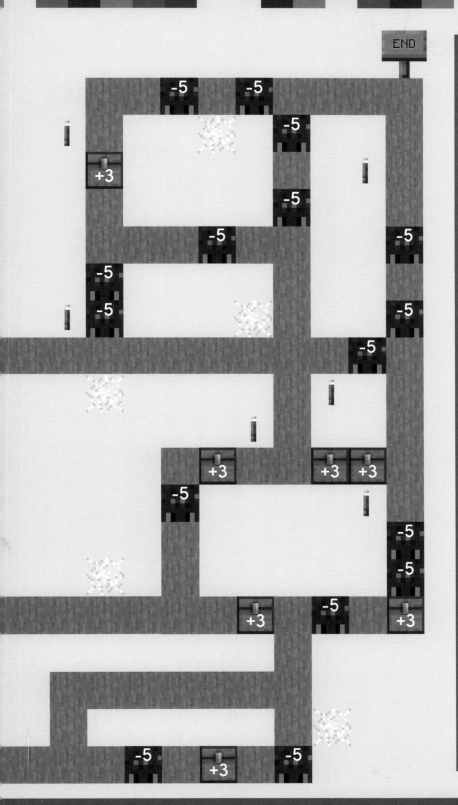

END

Track your values here!

25

-5 -5
-5
-5
-5
-5
-5
+3
-5
-5
-5
-5
+3
+3 +3
-5
-5
-5
-5
+3
-5
+3
-5
-5
+3

You did it! Place your sticker here.

MINECRAFT MISSION

The tunnel has led you to a huge deposit of ores. Collect it all with this mission!

This mission sends you on a search *inside* this book. There are items hidden in the top borders of most pages!

Search for pages that have **ore** (⬛ ⬛ ⬛) hidden at the top. Copy the numbers found on the ore into the row with the matching ore type below.

Subtract to find the total value of those ores.

Then take a deep breath. You did it!

15 - _____ = _____ ⬛

9 - _____ = _____ ⬛

20 - _____ - _____ = _____ ⬛

MINECRAFT
MINE

Great job! You earned a badge! Place your sticker here.

IT TAKES A VILLAGE

Once you encounter a village, you'll find villagers, iron golems, and cool items.

In this adventure, you will...

Encounter a village.

Open chests.

Identify professions.

Meet an iron golem.

Let's get started!

VOCABULARY

As you push through a stand of trees, you come across a village.

Find all the things you can do in a village in this word search. Words go up, down, across, and backward.

Find these words:

brew   plan   rest   run   shop   wait   work
craft   dig   eat   explore   farm   cook

M	A	C	R	A	F	T	R
F	P	W	K	E	W	S	E
A	L	E	E	G	A	H	S
R	A	R	A	I	I	O	T
M	N	B	T	D	T	P	W
E	X	P	L	O	R	E	O
F	R	I	E	R	U	N	R
K	O	O	C	N	D	S	K

When you're done, write the leftover letters at the bottom. They will spell something special you can do in a village.

_____ _____

MINECRAFT FACT: Villages are spread throughout the world and are home to helpful villagers.

44

Draw a line to connect the halves of each word, then write the full word in each space. Use the images in the box to help you.

You'll spell these items:

buc   mor   _____

ar   rt   _____

lant   ern   _____

bo   dle   _____

car   at   _____

ca   ket   _____

can   rot   _____

There are chests to open and special items to find.

Copy the letters from each chest into the spaces below.

You'll spell these items:

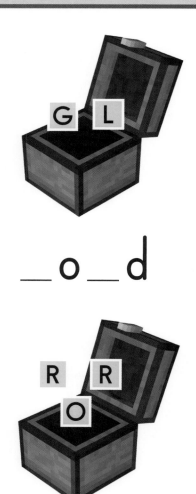

_ o _ d

_ p _ l _

a _ m _ _ _

_ _ _ o _

MINECRAFT FACT: Chests in villages hold good loot and helpful items.

There's a secret message hidden in these items. Use this guide to copy letters into the spaces below.

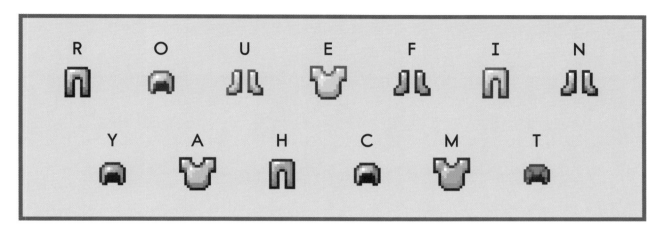

R   O   U   E   F   I   N
Y   A   H   C   M   T

_ _ _   _ _ _   _

_ _ _ _ _ _ _ _ _

_ _ _ _ !

Villagers have many different professions.

Write the profession under each villager. The letters around every circle spell one word. It's up to you to decide where to start.

Choose from these words:

> weaponsmith
> cartographer
>
> leatherworker
> mason
>
> librarian
> butcher

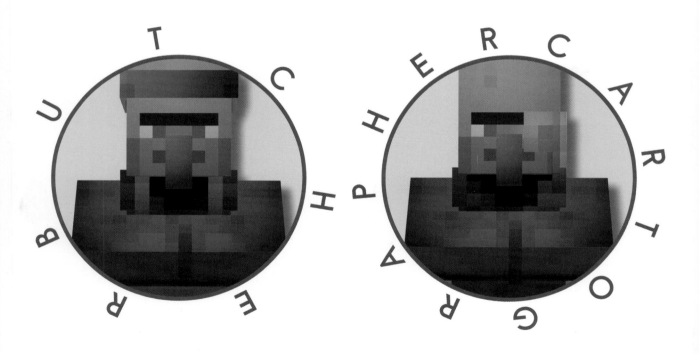

_____   _____

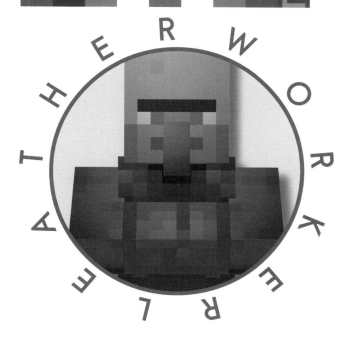

L E A T H E R W O R K E R

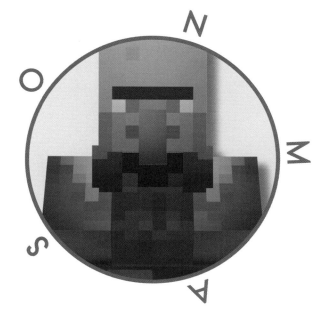

O N M A S O

T H W E A P O N S M I

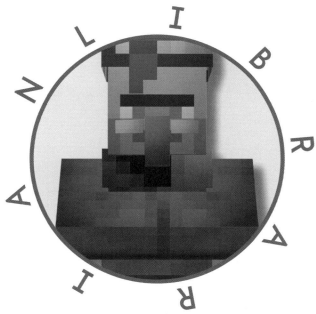

L I B R A R I A N

There's an iron golem in the village. It wants to be your friend.

Unscramble the letters and write the correct words in the spaces below the sign. Then read the golem's message.

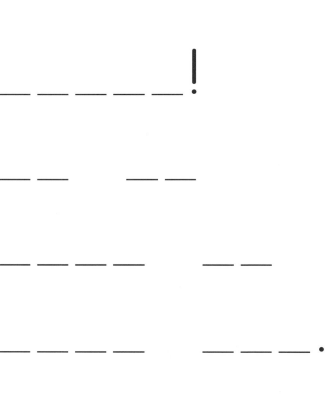

OHLLE TI SI ECNI
OT TMEE OYU

_ _ _ _ _ !

_ _   _ _

_ _ _ _   _ _

_ _ _ _ _   _ _ .

What do you say to an iron creature that keeps interrupting you?
"Golem away, I'm busy!"

Cross out one letter from each word to correct its spelling. The words are items that you can find and use in the village. The first one has been done for you.

aspple

berll

pegg

cahndle

goold

beid

bbread

buckket

zarrow

brrick

bozok

claye

carnrot

stuick

MINECRAFT MISSION

Your village is thriving now. It's a great place to meet up with your friends.

This mission is a project *outside* of this book! Make a game to play with a friend.

Make the game:

- Find crayons and index cards.
- Write each of these letters on separate cards:

T	E	F	A	H	I	L	C	M	T	E	Y	N	A	R	I	W	M	P
T	E	Y	N	A	R	I	W	M	P	T	E	F	A	H	I	L	C	M

- Shuffle the cards and deal five to each player.
- Put the rest of the cards in a pile, face down.

How to play:

- On your turn, draw one card.
- If you can spell one of these words with the cards you have, place them down in front of you:

play	mine	craft	with	me

- If you can't spell one of the five words, say a letter. If the other player has it, they must give that card to you. (If they have several, they only give you one.)
- Your turn ends when you ask for a letter and the other player doesn't have it. Then it is their turn.
- The first player to spell all five words and shout, "Play Minecraft with me!" is the winner.

MINECRAFT DISCOVER

Great job! You earned a badge! Place your sticker here.

MINECRAFT

TRADE

A FAIR TRADE

Villagers love to trade. It's a great way for you to get loot and level up.

In this adventure, you will...

Trade for emeralds.

Get armor.

Protect villagers.

Gain experience.

Let's get started!

You can trade all kinds of resources for emeralds.

Read the numbers next to each item and write the total value.

10 **+** 5 **=** _____

19 **+** 1 **=** _____

6 **+** 11 **=** _____

1 **+** 7  **+** 7 **=** _____

8 **+** 3 **+** 4  **=** _____

2 **+** 3 **+** 13 **=** _____

10 **+** 10 **+** 10 **+** 10 **=** _____

MINECRAFT FACT: The villagers' currency is emeralds.

Look at the number each villager is thinking. Circle emeralds below each villager so the total is equal to that number.

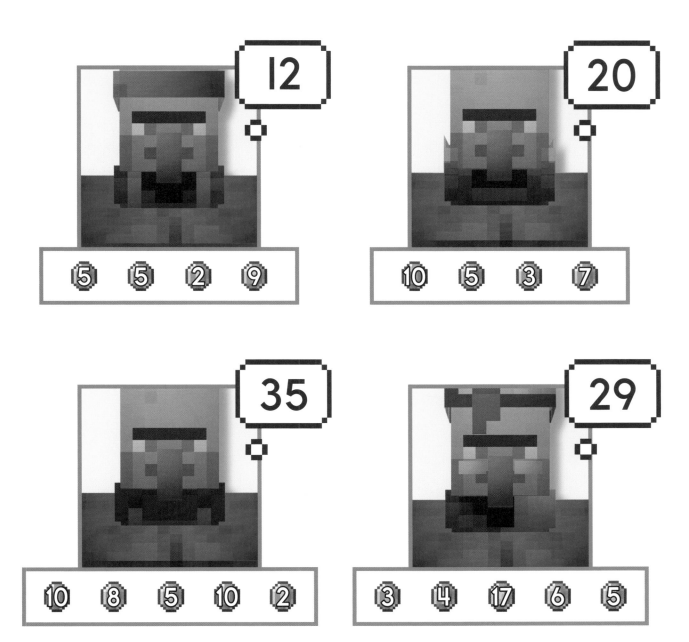

12

5 5 2 9

20

10 5 3 7

35

10 8 5 10 2

29

3 4 17 6 5

You can trade with a blacksmith to get armor.

Write how many emeralds you have left in each row.

10 — 4 = _____

50 / — 10 / = _____

18 — 11 = _____

17 — 2 — 2 = _____

18 — 3 — 5 = _____

20 / — 5 — 5 = _____

11 — 3 — 2 — 4 / = _____

MINECRAFT FACT: Some resources have better exchange values than others when trading with a villager.

Look at the number each villager is thinking. Cross out emeralds below each villager so the value of the leftover emeralds is equal to that number.

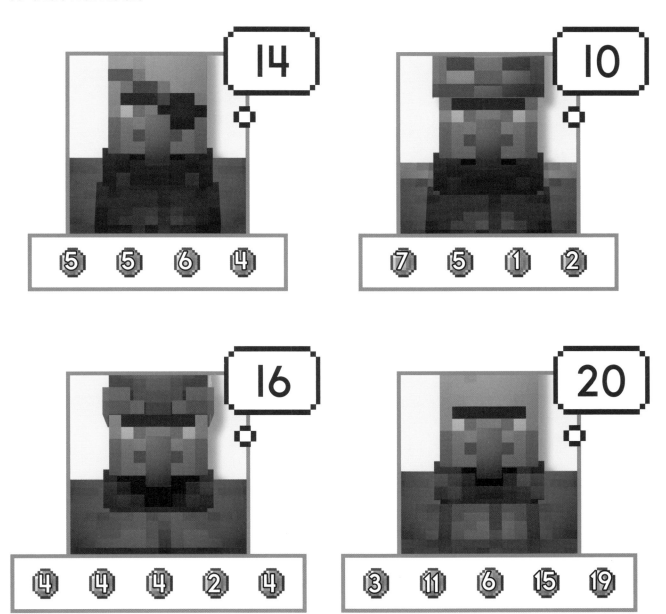

14

⑤ ⑤ ⑥ ④

10

⑦ ⑤ ① ②

16

④ ④ ④ ② ④

20

③ ⑪ ⑥ ⑮ ⑲

You've found a mason villager who wants to trade you some bricks. While you trade, keep an eye out for enemies that may be nearby.

Estimate how many bricks are in each group and circle that number. Use your best guess without counting!

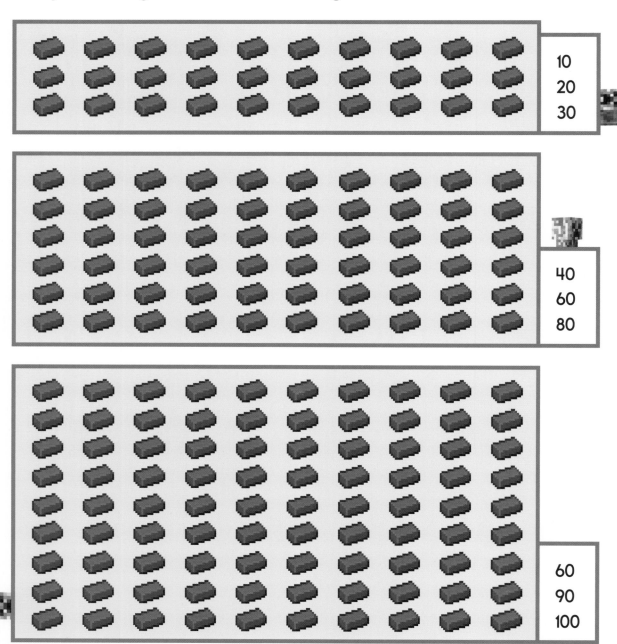

10
20
30

40
60
80

60
90
100

Without counting, guess how many villagers are on this page.

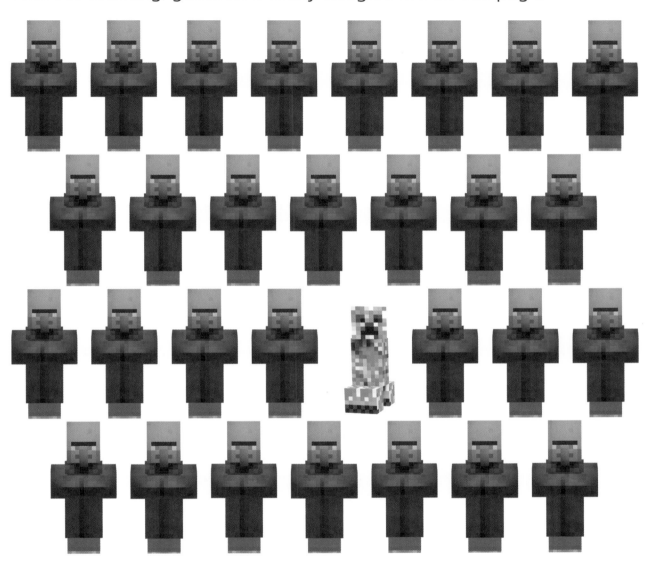

Write your guess here: _____

Now count all the villagers and write the exact number: _____

Was your guess higher or lower? Did you get it just right?

Wait! How many creepers are hiding on pages 58 and 59? _____

You did it! Place your sticker here.

As a reward for protecting the village from hostile mobs, you help yourself to items from some chests.

Find the total value of all the treasure in each chest. You'll have to **add (+)** *and* **subtract (-)**.

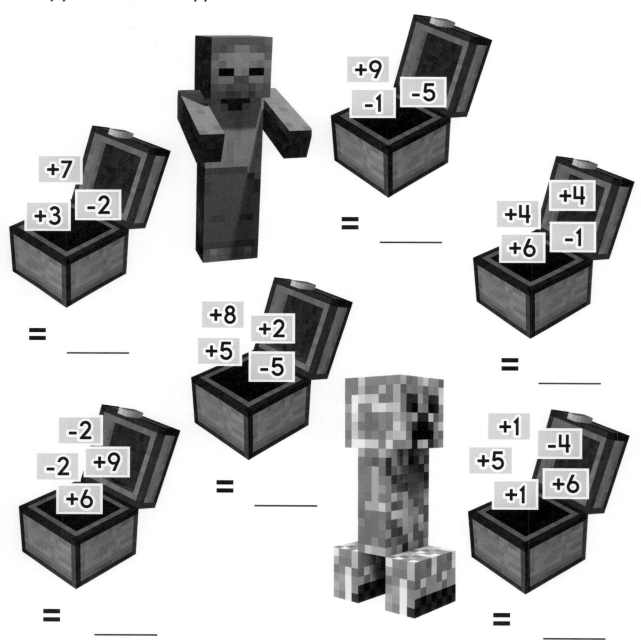

+9
-1   -5

= _____

+7
+3   -2

= _____

+4   +4
+6   -1

= _____

+8   +2
+5   -5

= _____

-2
-2   +9
+6

= _____

= _____

+1
+5   -4
+1   +6

= _____

What do you call a villager who makes you pay over and over again?   A bill-ager!

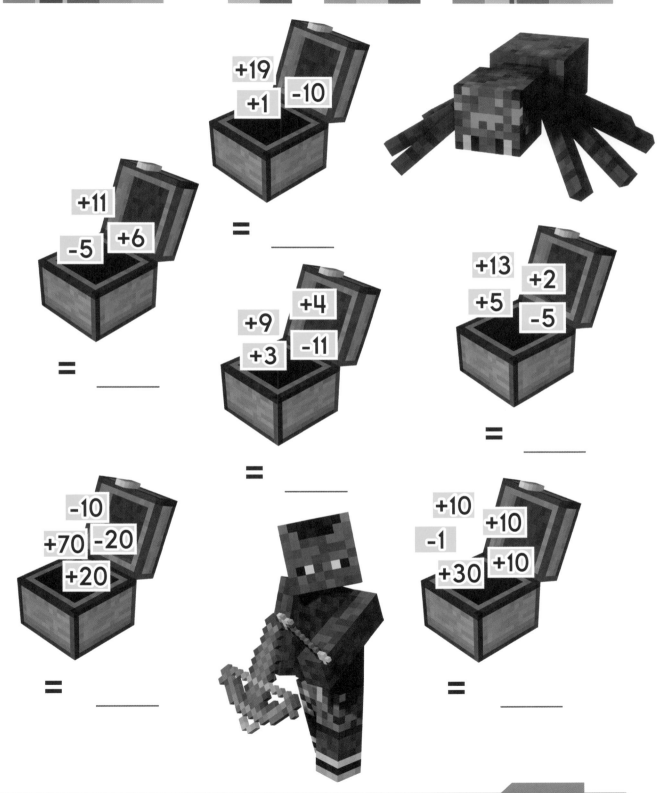

+19 +1 -10

= _____

+11 -5 +6

= _____

+9 +4 +3 -11

= _____

+13 +2 +5 -5

= _____

-10 +70 -20 +20

= _____

+10 +10 -1 +30 +10

= _____

MINECRAFT MISSION

The village was a great place to trade and gather items. Now try this mission to collect even better items.

This mission sends you on a search *inside* this book. There are items hidden in the top borders of most pages!

Search for pages that have **helmets** (🪖), **chestplates** (🛡), and **boots** (👢) hidden at the top.

Copy the number and its math symbol from each item into the spaces below. The first one has been done for you.

Total up the value and write the answer in the last space after the **equals (=)** symbol.

When you find the answer, give yourself that many cheers for completing the mission!

+10 ___ ___

___ ___ ___

= ___

MINECRAFT TRADE

Great job! You earned a badge! Place your sticker here.

62

FISH

You've reached an ocean. It's a great place to look for fish.

In this adventure, you will...

Craft a fishing pole.

Craft a boat.

Go fishing.

Find many types of fish.

GO FISH

Let's get started!

A fishing rod is a great tool for catching fish. Craft one with sticks and string.

Circle all the **lowercase** letters in these spiderwebs. Write the letters you've circled on the lines below to collect the string.

___ ___ ___ ___ ___ ___ ___   ___ ___ ___   ___ ___ ___ ___

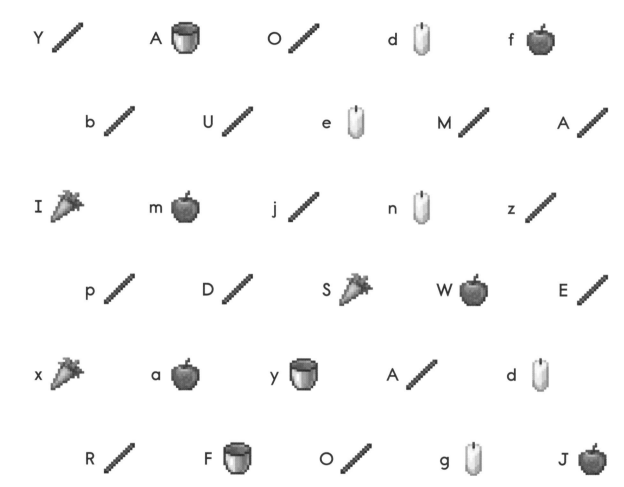

Circle all the sticks that have **uppercase** letters next to them. Write the letters you've circled on the lines below, then read the message. (Hint: Remember to only circle uppercase letters with sticks!)

Y · A · O · d · f

b · U · e · M · A

I · m · j · n · z

p · D · S · W · E

x · a · y · A · d

R · F · O · g · J

T · u · D · w · r

___ ___ ___ ___ ___ ___ ___ ___ ___ ___ ___ ___ !

You can see fish jumping farther out in the water! Craft a boat to reach them.

Circle the picture that makes sense with each sentence.

I gathered a lot of wood.

I got into my new boat.

 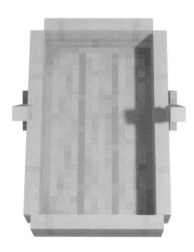

MINECRAFT FACT: Sometimes a fishing rod can catch treasure or junk instead of fish.

I saw more fish than dolphins.

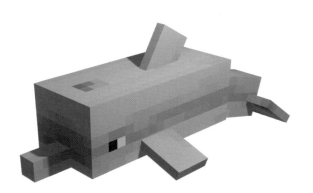 

Oops! I forgot to bring something to catch fish with.

The fish are biting. Use your pole to catch them.

Using the box below as a key, complete each sentence by adding the **punctuation mark** on the fish that is pictured.

Are you ready___

I know how to fish___

Hooray___ I caught one.

First___ ___ craft a rod___
Then___ ___ you can fish___

MINECRAFT FACT: Fish are a great food source and come in various species.

Using the key on page 68, draw a line from each rod to a fish whose punctuation mark makes each sentence correct.

Who are you___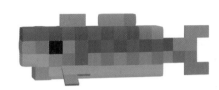

Look out___

Let's go eat___

Where is it___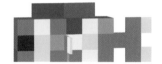

I like to fish___

Where can we go___

Run away___

Minecrafting makes you hungry. Collect a supply of many fish.

Find all the fish (and other animals) in this word search. Words go up, down, across, and backward.

Find these words:			
axolotl	squid	pufferfish	dolphin
salmon	turtle	clownfish	cod

H	S	I	F	R	E	F	F	U	P
N	H	A	A	Y	H	X	T	D	U
I	A	K	X	X	S	D	U	Y	P
H	I	S	Q	U	I	D	R	A	A
P	S	Z	F	A	F	L	T	X	C
L	A	A	Q	E	N	B	L	Y	O
O	L	S	A	D	W	B	E	L	D
D	M	U	L	T	O	L	O	X	A
S	O	S	W	Q	L	R	X	E	Z
J	N	H	D	C	C	C	O	F	X	J

How are Minecraft fish numbered? *Even and cod!*

Unscramble each word.

t s k
c i

_____

c a o
e
n

_____

i i g s
n f h

_____

a o b
t

_____

t e e u
r s a r

_____

MINECRAFT MISSION

While you were fishing, you discovered sunken treasure to share!

This mission sends you *outside* of this book! It's a scavenger hunt game you can make to play with a friend.

You'll need:

- A pencil
- Paper
- Six envelopes

How to play:

- Plan a hunt for a friend. It can be inside your house or around your backyard.

- Pick five places to hide your clues. Some good places are under a chair, behind a tree, or beside a book. (Don't make it too hard!)

- Write the five hiding places on pieces of paper. Put each one in an envelope and number them from one to five.

- Write "YOU WIN!" on a piece of paper and put it in the sixth envelope.

- Hand your friend envelope number one...and the hunt begins!

If you want to, you can let the winner of your scavenger hunt put the sticker on this page.

MINECRAFT

FISH

Great job! You earned a badge! Place your sticker here.

TEAM UP

Here come pillagers. You'll need powerful friends to stop them.

In this adventure, you will...

Dodge and block arrows.

Release iron golems.

Free allays.

Defeat the pillagers.

Let's get started!

Pillagers are shooting at you! Dodge and block their crossbow bolts and try to get across the field.

Begin at **START** and move either one space to the right or down.

Each time you land on a space, count the number of arrows. Then move that many spaces in a straight line: choose up, down, left, or right.

If your final move lands on a space that says "HIT!", color one shield on the chart below. If you still have blank shields on your chart, keep going and move one space in any direction. Otherwise, you must start over!

You'll have to lose a few shields to make it to **END**...but you can do it. Go!

ATTEMPT 1: 🛡 🛡 🛡 🛡

ATTEMPT 2: 🛡 🛡 🛡 🛡

ATTEMPT 3: 🛡 🛡 🛡 🛡

MINECRAFT FACT: Iron golems will fight alongside you against hostile mobs.

START	HIT!					HIT!
		HIT!		HIT!		
HIT!		HIT!	HIT!			HIT!
HIT!	HIT!			HIT!	HIT!	
		HIT!		HIT!	HIT!	
			HIT!			HIT!
		HIT!		HIT!		
	HIT!				HIT!	END

You did it! Place your sticker here.

You've found iron golems in cages. Set them free!

Circle the item that should come next in each line to continue the sequence.

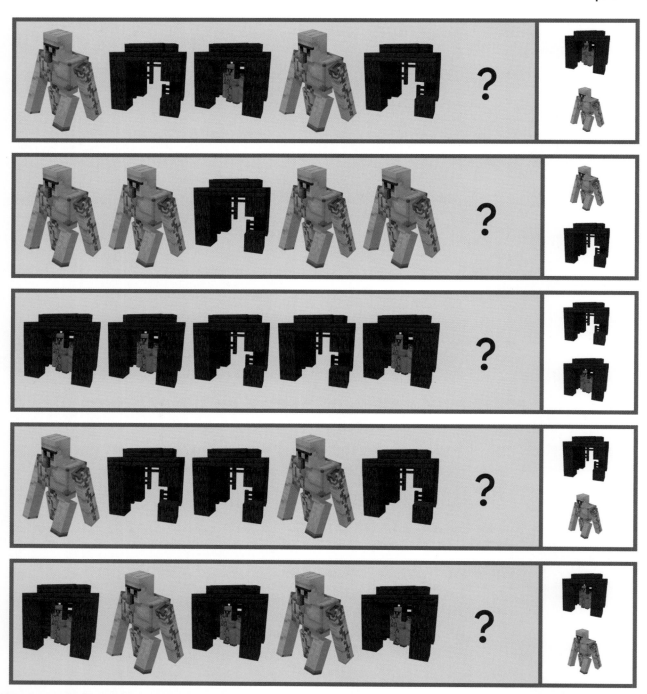

Pick one of the golems to continue each sequence and write its number in the correct space.

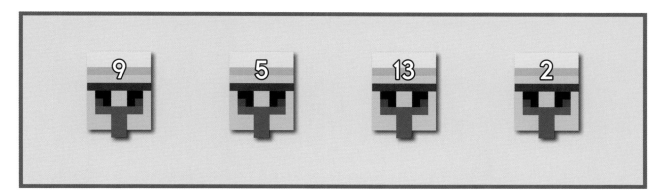

1	2	1	2	1	___
3	6	9	3	6	___
1	11	1	12	1	___
30	25	20	15	10	___

What is the total value of all your answers? _____

There are allays in cages, too. Set them free as well!

Write the symbol for either **greater than (>)** or **less than (<)** in each box.

3 ☐ 2   4 ☐ 6

6 ☐ 8   7 ☐ 3

5 ☐ 9   12 ☐ 9

15 ☐ 3

10 ☐ 2

10 ☐ 27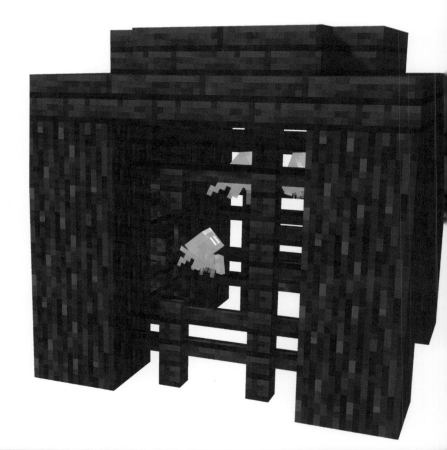

1 ☐ 989

0 ☐ 97

MINECRAFT FACT: Allays can help your defense by bringing you items you have dropped.

The allays brought math problems as gifts! Write the symbol for **greater than (>)**, **less than (<)**, or **equal to (=)** in each box.

2 ☐ 9

3 ☐ 8

16 ☐ 5

22 ☐ 22

150 ☐ 150

12 ☐ 11

10 ☐ 90

33 ☐ 33

16 ☐ 17

You did it! Place your sticker here.

Now that you have many friends at your side, you can rid the outpost of pillagers.

Write the symbol for either **addition (+)** or **subtraction (–)** in each box so that the numbers of villagers and pillagers are equal.

2 ☐ 17 = 19

33  ☐ 1 = 32

14  ☐ 6 = 20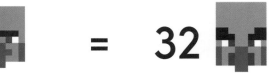

8 ☐ 1  = 11 ☐ 2

17 ☐ 6  = 10 ☐ 1

20 ☐ 10 = 5 ☐ 5

What did the fighter do when everyone applauded?
He took a cross-bow!

Follow each trail. Start with the number below each hero. **Add (+)** or **subtract (-)** and write your new value as you pass each item or pillager along the way. Then write the final totals at the end of each trail.

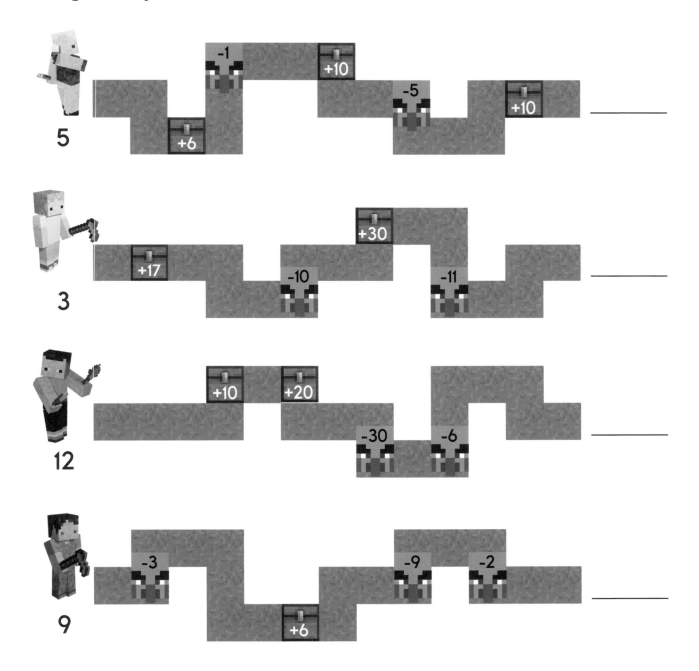

MINECRAFT MISSION

Head back to the village with your companions. Make sure no enemies are sneaking along with you.

This mission sends you on a search *inside* this book. There are items hidden in the top borders of most pages!

Search for **skeletons** (☐). Each one has a letter on it.

If the page number where it appears is **even**, don't worry about that skeleton.

If the page number is **odd**, write the letter in one of the spaces below.

___ ___ ___ ___ ___

___ ___ ___ ___

Now unscramble those letters into the spaces below to spell where you are now.

S___ ___ ___ A___ H___ ___ ___

MINECRAFT TEAM UP

Great job! You earned a badge! Place your sticker here.

DEFEND

PILLAGER ATTACK!

Pillagers have entered a village. It's up to you to stop them.

In this adventure, you will...

Ring the bell.

Board up doors.

Summon more iron golems.

Battle!

Let's get started!

Ring the bell to alert all the villagers that they are under attack.

Circle the word that makes each sentence grammatically correct.

Pillagers | is are | coming!

Did you hear? I just | rang ring | the bell.

Let's find a | place places | to hide.

You should | be are | safe inside.

I hope there | are am | not too many enemies.

I will protect | we you |.

MINECRAFT FACT: The bell at the center of a village warns villagers of a threat and tells them to get indoors.

Use one of the words in the box to fill in each sentence.

is	have	fun	be	will	to

It _____ time to battle.

Don't _____ scared.

I _____ some friends who will help.

Everything _____ be okay.

I am ready _____ fight!

This will be _____.

The villagers have run into their homes for safety. Board up all the doors to protect them.

Circle the correct word for each sentence.

Block this door doors .

There are villager villagers inside.

The pillager pillagers are scaring them.

These fence fences should keep them out.

I hope no mob mobs gets us.

I'm glad these home homes are solid.

MINECRAFT FACT: When villagers are safe inside buildings, a blocked door will keep mobs out.

These words are all singular or plural. Cross out the word in each box that does not belong.

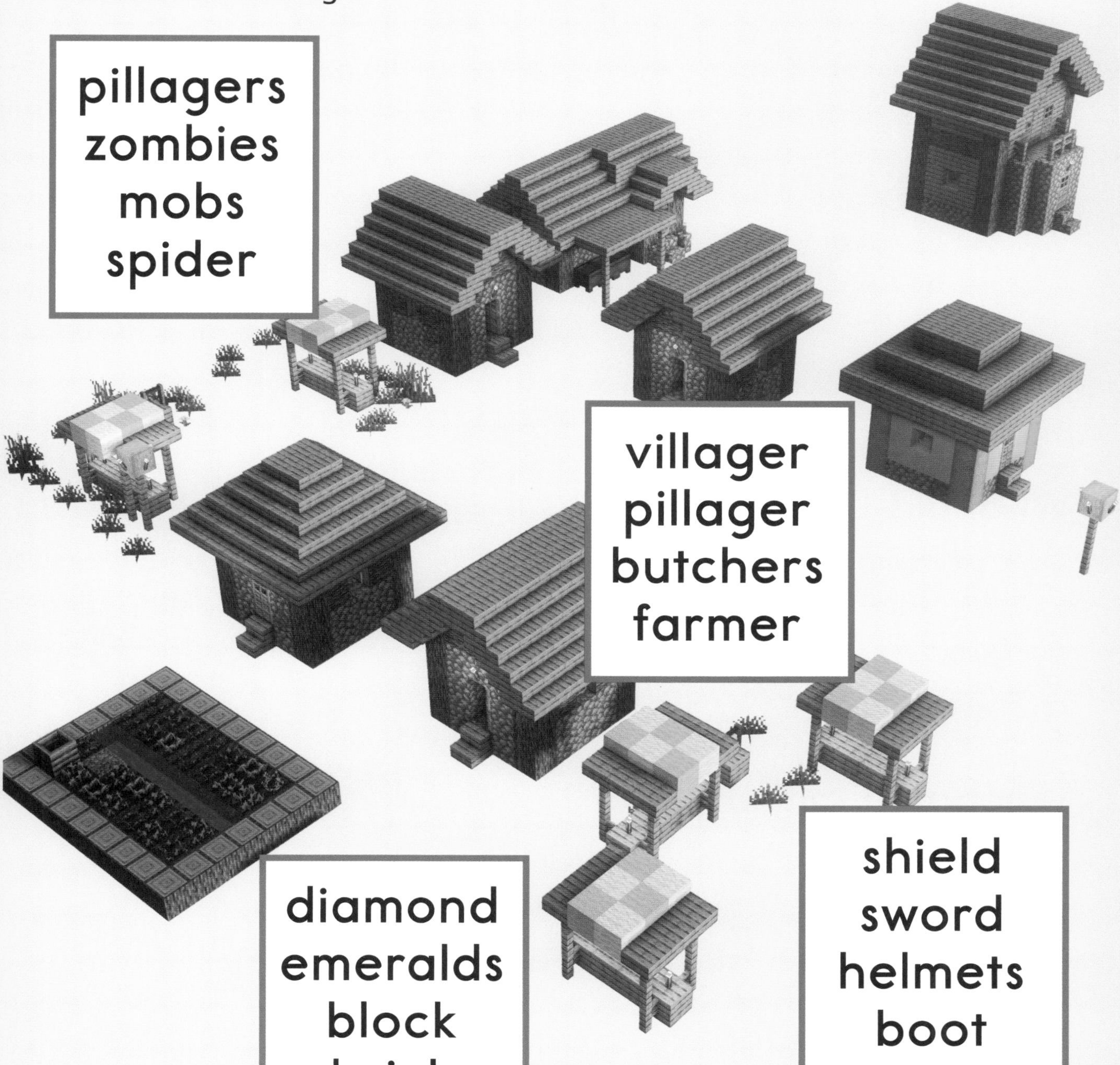

pillagers
zombies
mobs
spider

villager
pillager
butchers
farmer

diamond
emeralds
block
brick

shield
sword
helmets
boot

You did it! Place your sticker here.

It's going to take all your skills to save this village. It's a good thing you have iron golems to help you!

Read each sentence. Then circle the answer to the question.

I found some heavy iron blocks.

What were they made of? | blocks iron bees |

I saw three pillagers walking uphill.

What did I see? | fish golems pillagers |

I used a carved pumpkin to make an iron golem.

What did I make? | lantern golem piglin |

Do not go in that cave! It is full of spiders.

Should I go in there? | yes no |

MINECRAFT FACT: You'll earn loot by saving villagers.

Oh no! I don't see anyone else around.

What best describes me? | happy fast alone |

It's getting dark. I wish I had something that gave off light.

What do I need? | sword torch block |

I need to get the treasure at the other side of this lake.

Which of these will help me? | ladder helmet boat |

It is so dark! Those creepers look like they want to battle.

What do the enemies want to do? | fight chase dig |

You did it! Place your sticker here.

With iron golems at your side, smash the pillagers!

Follow this stony path from **START** to **END**. You can pick any path you want. Write each word that you pass in the spaces below.

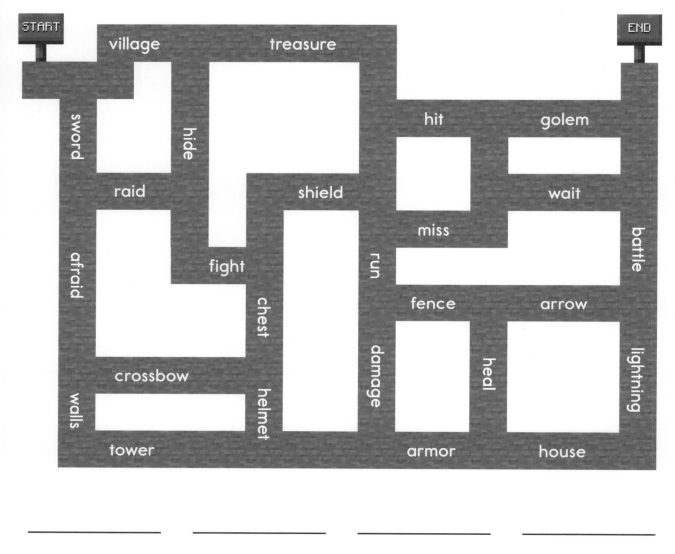

START							END
village	treasure			hit	golem		
sword	hide						
raid		shield			wait		battle
afraid			miss				
fight		run	fence	arrow			
chest		damage	heal	lightning			
walls	crossbow	helmet					
tower			armor	house			

_____   _____   _____   _____

_____   _____   _____   _____

_____   _____   _____   _____

What kind of pants can alert villagers?   *Bell bottoms!*

90

Now write a story that includes as many of the words you passed in the maze as you can.

Draw a picture of what happened in your story.

You did it! Place your sticker here.

MINECRAFT MISSION

You're a hero! You saved the village.

Now try one last mission _outside_ of this book, and imagine what your world would be like if you lived in Minecraft.

Use some of the five prompts below to tell your story, or go off on your own and describe a fun adventure.

You can write with a fancy pen or your favorite crayon on a separate piece of paper. Once you've written your ideas, read them out loud to your friends and family and see what they think!

When I woke up today, I discovered my house was full of...

I looked for parents, but they had turned into...

When I went outside, I found that I was in a Minecraft...

My friends were all...

I rescued everyone by crafting a...

MINECRAFT

DEFEND

Great job! You earned a badge! Place your sticker here.

ANSWERS

Pages 4–5

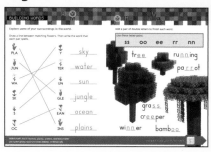

Pages 6–7

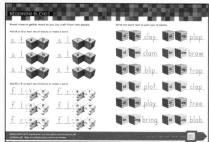

Pages 8–9

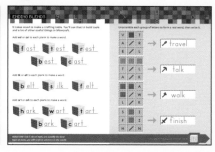

Pages 10–11

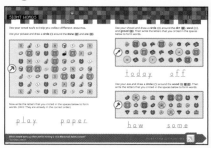

Pages 14–15

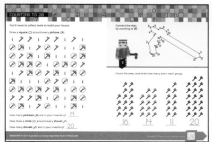

Pages 16–17

Pages 18–19

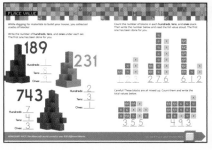

Pages 20–21

Page 22

Pages 24–25

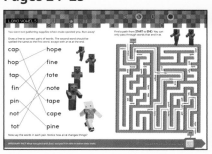

Pages 26–27

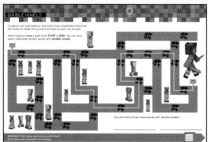

Pages 28–29

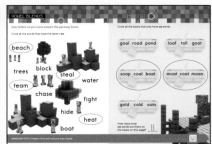

Pages 30–31

Pages 34–35
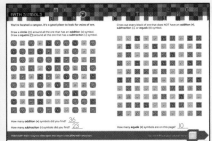

Pages 36–37

Pages 38–39
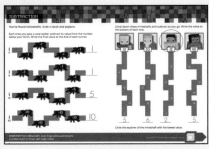

Page 42

Pages 44–45
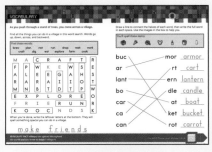

Pages 46–47

Pages 48–49
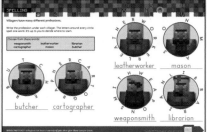

Pages 50–51

Pages 54–55
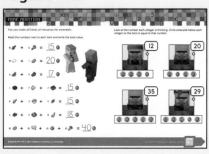

Pages 56–57
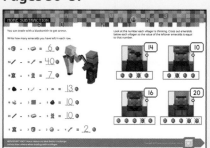

Pages 58–59
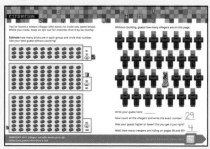

Pages 60–61
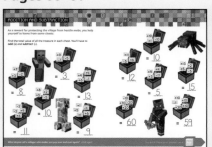

Page 62

Pages 64–65
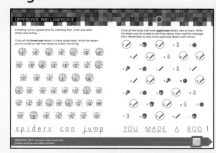

Pages 66–67

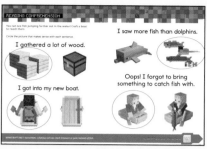

Pages 68–69

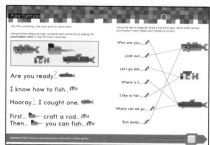

Pages 70–71

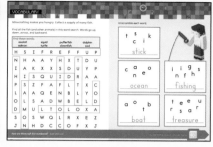

Pages 76–77

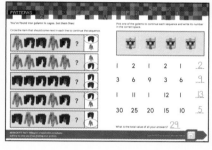

Pages 78–79

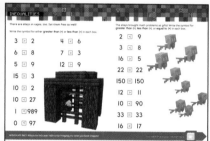

Pages 80–81

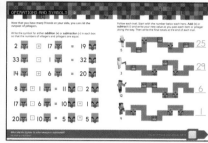

Page 82

Pages 84–85

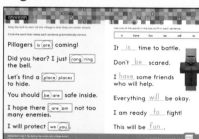

Pages 86–87

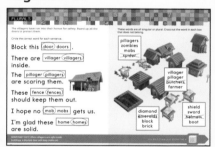

Pages 88–89

MINECRAFT ACHIEVEMENT

Let it be known throughout the Overworld:

_____

YOUR NAME

has completed an adventure filled with **MINECRAFT MISSIONS!**

GRADE 1

MINECRAFT MINECRAFT

MINECRAFT

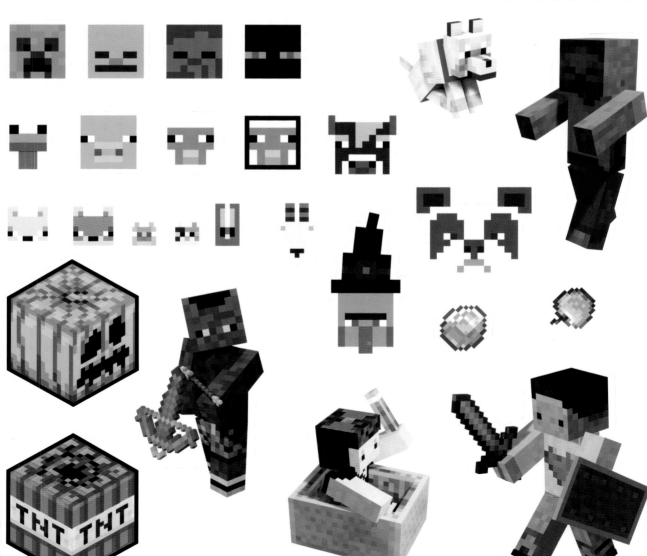

TNT TNT

MINECRAFT DEFEND

MINECRAFT TEAM UP

MINECRAFT FISH

MINECRAFT TRADE

MINECRAFT DISCOVER

MINECRAFT EXPLORE

MINECRAFT BUILD

MINECRAFT SURVIVE

MINECRAFT MINE